RealityShifters® Guide to

High Energy Money

by Cynthia Sue Larson

RealityShifters® is a registered trademark of Cynthia Sue Larson

No part of this publication may be reproduced, stored in a retrieval system, or transmitted in any form or by any means, electronic, mechanical, photocopying, recording, scanning, or otherwise, except as permitted under Section 107 or 108 of the 1976 United States Copyright Act, without either the prior written permission of the Publisher, or authorization through payment of the appropriate per-copy fee to the Copyright Clearance Center, Inc., 222 Rosewood Drive, Danvers, MA 01923, 978-750-8400, fax 978-646-8600, or on the web at www.copyright.com. Address Publisher Requests to RealityShifters, P.O. Box 7393, Berkeley, CA 94707-7393.

Limit of Liability/ Disclaimer of Warranty: While the publisher and author have used their best efforts in preparing this book, they make no representations or warranties with respect to the accuracy or completeness of the contents of this book and specifically disclaim any implied varieties of merchantability or fitness for a particular purpose. No warranty may be created or extended by sales representatives or written sales materials. The advice and strategies contained herein may not be suitable for your situation. You should consult with a professional where appropriate. Neither the publisher nor author shall be liable for any loss of profit or any other commercial damages, including but not limited to special, incidental, consequential or other damages. Techniques, ideas, and suggestions in this book are not intended as a substitute for financial or medical advice. Any application of the techniques, ideas and suggestions in this book is at the reader's sole discretion and risk.

RealityShifters Guide to High Energy Money
ISBN-13: 978-1456465629
ISBN-10: 1456465627
By Cynthia Sue Larson
Cover Artwork by: Tessala Larson
Copyright @ 2010 -- Cynthia Sue Larson
Printed in the USA
Published: December 2010
Printed by: CreateSpace

CONTENTS:

Introduction 1
Money as Energy 5
High Energy Money Stories 14
Energizing Money 22
Money Self-Assessment 33
Improving Your Relationship with Money .. 43
Finding Money 50
Keeping Money 61
Growing Money 71
Conclusion 79
Bibliography 82
About the Author 84

*Dedicated to the experience of
prosperity for everyone*

Introduction

What exactly is High Energy Money? Is it money on steroids, accelerated money, or money with such an intense buzz that people feel electrified just being close to it? In a way, the answers to all these questions could be, "yes," but what makes this subject so interesting is that there is a reason some money can feel so tremendously energized.

The secret to understanding High Energy Money rests not so much in noticing what it is about this money that is so special, as in activating an energized relationship between money and ourselves. When we gain confidence and experience in positively interacting with money, and replace negative patterns of thoughts and feelings with positive ones, we can reap great financial rewards.

Money is something that most of us desire more of, many of us feel nervous about, and some of us feel we don't fully understand, so there is a lot of room for most of us to improve our relationship with money. Researchers conducting a survey for Allianz Life Insurance in June 2010 were surprised to discover that 61% of the respondents between the ages of 44 to 75 feared running out of money more than they feared dying. This level of fear was much greater than anticipated, even though the survey was conducted during an economic recession, and helps to illustrate the point that most of us could benefit from an improved relationship with money.

When our relationship with money is optimally aligned, we can more easily discover new sources of money, keep more of the money that comes our way, and steadily increase our savings... in any economic climate. A better understanding of the energy of money provides us with a deeper sense of respect for the way we interact with it, and the way our thoughts and feelings influence our financial reality.

The High Energy Money concept is based on the principle that our thoughts and feelings literally change the physical world. When we are feeling happy in our relationship with money, we can become increasingly confident re-envisioning what money means to us and how to best work with and enjoy it. When we are feeling in harmony with High Energy Money, we can take responsibility for infusing a sense of infectious optimism into our intentions for money, adopting an attitude of consistently asking the Universe each day,

"How good can life get?" and

"What can I best do right now to help make my life as good as it can be?"

The power of these questions is that we are now poised to notice answers to questions we would most enjoy getting answers to. Everywhere our attention turns, we are actively looking for opportunities for improvement, and ideas for solving problems in ways that benefit us all.

While my Masters of Business Administration (MBA) degree provides me with a background in comprehending matters of finance, accounting and good business practices primarily based in rational, left-brain thought, this *RealityShifters guide to High Energy Money* is intended to present an optimal balance between rational / methodical and intuitive / creative thought. This book is intended to help us have fun enjoying good feelings about money at the same time as we steadily develop a sense of pride in our financial prowess.

This book is created to help you with two basic goals:

- Open your mind to the possibilities of what money can be and do for you at its highest levels of vibration, and

- Understand and improve your personal relationship with money.

High Energy Money is all about inviting ourselves on a journey to find out how exciting, wonderful, and rewarding our relationship with money can be.

There is a perfect question to keep in mind as you read this book, and after you've set it down that will continuously assist you in expanding your idea of what is possible. You can set your intention to experience the very best financial situation imaginable by asking:

> *"How good can
> my relationship with money get?!"*

Money as Energy

"Money was never a big motivation for me, except as a way to keep score. The real excitement is playing the game." —Donald Trump

Physicists tell us that <u>everything</u> is energy, but sometimes it seems money is doubly so. Those who have lots of money seem to have a knack for keeping and building financial savings, while others who've been very poor all their lives emit an entirely different vibe. These energy vibes are something you can sense when meeting people for the first time, or when spending time in their homes or at their workplaces. You can immediately get a sense of the presence or absence of confidence they feel about life in general, and money in particular based on how nervous or comfortable they seem to feel when discussing financial matters. Peoples' attitudes of expectation of either a positive or a disappointing future is one which sets the stage for how people respond when opportunity comes knocking at their doors. Those who think optimistically are poised to consider new ideas, while those who feel fearful or down-trodden tend to resist new ideas.

One secret that those rabbit-pulling financial wizards know that other people don't is that we don't so much *find* High Energy Money as *make* it. We make money by putting a great deal of our own energy, thought and passion into projects we can feel passionately enthusiastic and involved with. While it is true that amazing financial opportunities sometimes come along for people to get rich quick with little to no time, effort or energy on their part, most too-good-to-be-true schemes are precisely that.

Learning to take carefully measured risks again and again, and revising financial strategy to pick successful investments more often than not over the long run is what "The Oracle of Omaha," Warren Buffett does far better than most. What Buffet looks for in companies he chooses to invest in is to "buy certainties at a discount," where those certainties are defined by the predictability of a given business' economic situation. Buffett is famous for only investing in companies that are within his "circle of confidence," meaning that he does a great deal of research first, to discover how well a particular business is doing and has done in the past, as well as how it compares to similar comparable businesses, before he invests.

In addition to improving our rational analysis of how best to invest, we can benefit from infusing our finances with clear intentions and positive attitude for success. These positive intentions make a big difference, whether we are workers who ensure our savings exceed our expenses, or investors who ensure positive returns on investment capital.

Rags-to-riches entrepreneur Thomas Chen "came to America to find opportunity," from his native country of Taiwan in August 1982, when he was 27 years old. By 2003, Chen was president and one of the cofounders of Crystal Window and Door Systems, which posted $42 million in sales in 2002. Chen's intentions help explained how he energizes his financial success. "After a point, the money isn't important. You want your dream to keep going. I want to keep expanding our business. The second dream is to create more jobs and to give back to the community."

There is an energy of money that leaves people feeling charged up and joyful when giving it away. Researchers at the University of British Columbia and the Harvard Business School found that people are significantly, measurably happier when they spend money "pro-socially" on gifts for others and on charitable donations, rather than spending it on themselves. University of British Columbia Assistant Professor Elizabeth Dunn stated, "These findings suggest that very minor alterations in spending allocations – as little as $5 – may be enough to produce real gains in happiness on a given day."

We can feel a sense of high energy when contemplating multi-million dollar businesses, and wonder if money always had such a sense of power and energy to it. A look back at the history of money provides us with some surprising insights into the many forms of money used by mankind around the world.

Right from the very beginning, people infused energy into money, so whatever currency was being used became much more than what first met the eye. Livestock, such as cattle and grains were some of the earliest forms of money, dating back as far as 9,000 BC. Many cultures created a basis for money with complex trade arrangements involving shells, carved stones or sticks, or other semi-precious objects that represented socially accepted and agreed upon value. These early types of money were then understood to be worth a certain number of sheep or fish, for example, and yet were easier to transport or store than the sheep or fish they could be exchanged for. Other types of early money prior to coins included: salt, tobacco, liquor, tea, spears, honey, round stones, animal skins, blankets, gemstones, and shark teeth. With the advent of banking in ancient Mesopotamia circa 3,000 BC, people were finally able to feel a sense of safety with placing their wealth somewhere other than right nearby, and acceptable deposits in these first banks included grains, precious metals, and tools. The first coin money was created in 687 BC in Lydia from stamped nuggets of electrum, a naturally occurring amalgam of gold and silver, and featured the mark of a roaring lion.

I've been amazed to see the vast variation in money in countries I have visited around the world, with some of the most unusual coins being the gigantic stone coins on the island of

Yap in Micronesia in the Pacific Ocean. All of the stone money I saw on Yap was bigger and heavier than I was, and even though the stone wheels were round, I was awestruck to contemplate how they could ever be moved. In a moment, my whole world view of money was transformed, since Yap money did not fit in anyone's pocket, nor could it easily be hidden or tucked away. I had no idea how it could ever be possible to spend such money, or to get change in return for purchases.

William Henry Furness, an American anthropologist, wrote about the Yap islanders' monetary system in his book, *The Island of Stone Money*, "Their medium of exchange they call *fei*, and it consists of large, solid, thick, stone wheels, ranging in diameter from a foot to twelve feet, having in the centre a hole varying in size with the diameter of the stone, wherein a pole may be inserted sufficiently large and strong to bear the weight and facilitate transportation. These stone "coins" were originally quarried and shaped and brought to Uap by some venturesome native navigators, in canoes and on rafts." Furness continues to explain a most intriguing aspect of this monetary system, in that a "noteworthy feature of this stone currency… is that it is not necessary for its owner to reduce it to possession. After concluding a bargain that involves the price of a *fei* too large to be conveniently moved, its new owner is quite content to accept the bare acknowledgment of ownership and without so much as a mark to indicate the exchange, the coin remains undisturbed on the former owner's premises. My faithful old friend, Fatumak, assured me that there was in the village near-by a family whose wealth was unquestioned – acknowledged by every one – and yet no one, not even the family itself, had ever laid eye or hand on this wealth; it consisted of an enormous *fei*, whereof the size is known only by tradition; for the past two or three generations it had been, and at that very time it was lying at the bottom of the sea! Many years ago an ancestor of this family, on an expedition after *fei*, secured this remarkably large and exceedingly valuable stone, which was placed on a raft to be towed homeward. A violent storm arose, and the party, to save their lives, were obliged to cut the raft adrift, and the stone sank out of sight. When they reached home, they all testified that the *fei* was of magnificent proportions and of extraordinary quality, and that it was lost through no fault of the owner. Thereupon it was universally conceded in their simple faith that the mere accident of its loss overboard was too trifling to mention, and that a few hundred feet of water off shore ought not to affect its marketable value, since it was all chipped out in proper form. The purchasing power of that stone remains, therefore, as valid as if it were leaning visibly against the side of the owner's house."

Another interesting tale from the island of Yap is relayed by Furness, "There are no wheeled vehicles on Uap and, consequently, no cart roads; but there have always been clearly defined paths communicating with the different settlements. When the German Government assumed the ownership of The Caroline Islands, after the purchase of them from Spain in 1898, many of these paths or highways were in bad condition, and the chiefs of the several districts were told that they must have them repaired and put in good order. The roughly dressed blocks of coral were, however, quite good enough for the bare feet of the natives; and many were the repetitions of the command, which still remained unheeded. At last it was decided to impose a fine for disobedience on the chiefs of the districts. In what shape was the fine to be levied? ... At last, by a happy thought, the fine was exacted by sending a man to every *failu* and *pahai* throughout the disobedient districts, where he simply marked a certain number of the most valuable *fei* with a cross in black paint to show that the stones were claimed by the government. This instantly worked like a charm; the people, thus dolefully impoverished, turned to and repaired the highways to such good effect from one end of the island to the other, that they are now like park drives. Then the government dispatched its agents and erased the crosses. Presto! The fine was paid, the happy *failus* resumed possession of their capital stock, and rolled in wealth."

The interesting thing about considering various types of monetary systems is that we can see in the ways people ascribe value to different tokens of wealth how we are recognizing an energy charge in the money. Money is not the paper or coin or stone it is printed on, so much as it is the idea of something of value that can be exchanged for valuable goods and services.

While it's long been said that emotions are "energy in motion," much the same can be said about money. Whenever money flows, there is a lot going on, whereas wherever money is stuck or not moving, not much is happening. What has not been so well understood is the way we are able to energize money… and get it moving for us.

Fun with Money: A Check for You!

Write a check to yourself for an amount of money you believe could possibly come your way by a certain day "made payable to" your name, from "The Universe." Be sure to include a specific amount of money and date, and keep this check exactly where you keep other checks and income. Every time you look at this check, feel the joy you'll experience when this money arrives in the form of a real check!

Fun with Money: Million Dollar Bill

Put a "Million Dollar Bill" of play money in your wallet as a way to remind yourself that you always have lots of cash on hand, and help yourself feel comfortable and relaxed with that idea. Your Million Dollar Bill can be easy and affordable -- you can print an image from the Internet, or purchase one at a toy store.

High Energy Money Stories

There was a terrible time in billionaire Donald Trump's life when he owed creditors billions of dollars that he was unable to pay. While walking through the New York streets on his way to a meeting with those creditors, Trump passed a bum in the street and realized with a sense of shock that this bum "was worth $9.2 billion more than I was." While such an epiphany was initially unnerving, this revelation led Trump to consider how his creditors were wishing for him to succeed just as much as he wished it for himself, a realization which gave him insights as to how best he might renegotiate the terms of his loans when he reached his meeting. Indeed, this very revelation of Trump's was in fact, an energization of money… of the money he had borrowed, which he was confident would be put to work effectively in ways many others including himself would later profit from.

We can learn a great deal from High Energy Money stories from business owners like Donald Trump, as well as from people who make a transition from being employees to business owners… taking some chances in order to see their dreams come true. More importantly, these success stories generally feature a sense of confidence and enthusiasm in future financial prospects – an energization of the money involved and invested.

Cardboard Scraps to Coffee Riches

American inventor Jay Sorenson found himself floundering after the company that owned the gas station he managed in Portland, Oregon moved out of town. Real estate dabbling showed Sorenson he "wasn't very good at it," and he wondered how he could possibly support his family. One day, he spilled coffee on his lap, and thought, "there had to be a better way," as he noted how coffee house customers were precariously and gingerly holding steaming-hot cups between thumb and forefinger to avoid getting burned.

Sorenson invented and developed a cardboard sleeve to fit around the coffee cups, and offered it to Starbucks, who replied that they wanted exclusive rights, as they moved rather slowly toward making a fair and equitable offer. Sorenson opted to borrow funds from his parents and credit cards to hire a patent attorney and found his company, Java Jacket, to create the first 100,000 coffee cup jackets from waffled, recycled cardboard. Sorenson fortuitously learned about a coffee trade show at one coffee shop where he sold some of his first products there for the money he needed in order to attend the trade show, where he then took orders from 150 cafes.

While Sorenson took big, scary risks on a new business idea at a time when he had no source of income but continued to have ongoing expenses, his faith in his vision and his consistently positive, results-oriented mindset brought him phenomenal success. Sorenson believed in his business idea, thereby energizing his investment funds and every aspect of his budding operations. By 2003, Java Jacket sold between 20 million and 25 million sleeves a month, and now supports numerous charities including Make-A-Wish Foundation, the Humane Society of the United States, and Coffee Kids.

Rags to riches stories are immensely popular, because they give us hope that no matter how hard our lives may be right now, we can overcome almost any obstacles when we have a goal in mind, and when we maintain a commitment to investing our own time, effort and energy in helping do something that in some way makes the world a better place.

Our comprehension that reality shifts with changes in our thoughts and feelings is central to an appreciation for how we can change our financial situation miraculously in a moment, just as easily as we might envision and then find a perfect parking place precisely when and where we need it most. "Shifts happen" for real and very often in ways that might seem completely impossible, if we didn't see it for ourselves.

As you read the following stories of reality shifts involving money, please keep in mind how any and all of these money shifts could you.

Dollar Bills Appear tc Waitress

I was at the Chevy's Fresh Mex restaurant in Alameda with my daughters one evening when I noticed I did not have enough dollar bills for the tip I wished to leave. I showed my daughter sitting next to me how my wallet only contained two one dollar bills, and then I closed my wallet, commenting to her that it would really be nice if more dollar bills would show up in my wallet. After a moment, I opened my wallet and looked inside it once again with my daughter, and we found two more one dollar bills! I closed my wallet again and asked my daughter, "Should I look again for another dollar bill?" and grinned as she nodded "Yes!" enthusiastically... and the next time I opened my wallet, there was another dollar bill. We repeated this process of me closing my wallet and grinning as I asked "Should I look again?" and my daughters agreed – as I pulled out a total of six one dollar bills one at a time – more than enough for the tip!

One Thousand Dollars Appears

After attending one of my workshops about auras and energy in Sacramento, California, and having read my book *Aura Advantage* and listening to the *Aura Healing Meditations* CD, a man was shocked to see one day that

...er $1,000 mysteriously appeared in one of ...is desk drawers. He was amazed to inform me, "It appeared in an obvious place, so I don't think I could have possibly "over looked" it. This was a truly remarkable reality shift."

That man's amazing experience later prompted me to realize that if $1,000 could appear in cash in a drawer, it could just as easily appear in a bank account. At the time, I was dreaming about taking a vacation that cost about $1,000 more than what I had in my vacation fund, so I really loved this idea, and put some positive energy into visualizing how happy I'd be to discover an extra $1,000 more than I thought I had in my bank account. One day, *voila!* I noticed that I did indeed have $1,000 more in my bank checking account than what I had before. There were no signs that it had been added to my account through a deposit or series of deposits, but instead it appeared as if it had always been there. Best of all, this windfall allowed me to enjoy some much needed vacation time relaxing… knowing the entire time that money really can simply materialize.

Lottery Jackpot Winners

In January 2002, Jodi and Patrick Southard were suffering through a financial crisis of ballooning expenses, as they had switched to a bi-weekly mortgage schedule that demanded they pay three house payments in 45 days at the same time as they needed to pay outstanding holiday bills. In February, the transmission in their truck blew up. "It felt like we were in a hole and the more we dug out, the more it caved in," Jodi recalls. Fortunately for the Southards, they won New Jersey's "Pick 6" Lottery Jackpot in May 2002, and chose to take $4 million in cash. The Southards were overjoyed to have such a welcome windfall of cash, and the means to pay for their children's college education.

We can see a common thread in most stories of amazingly, miraculously good fortune with money. There is often a sense of need for the money at the time, yet also a somewhat relaxed state of mind regarding whether any money would be coming in. A relaxed, positive, open state of mind is optimal... and if circumstances are difficult, a great sense of optimism is helpful despite the challenges and problems being faced.

After reading these stories about discovering money unexpectedly, have fun letting your imagination run wild, as you consider other places and ways you might enjoy finding money coming into your life. What I've noticed regarding miraculous money manifestation is that it seems to come through best when invited... so taking some time now to imagine such a thing happening to you is time well spent.

Imagine what it might feel like to receive an unexpectedly large sum of cash – how much good will you do for others with the money that comes your way? When you know that the money is not just for you, but also to bring joy and happiness to others, you may find the notion of receiving such money a little easier to contemplate.

Think about how open you are to receiving money coming your way as if out of the blue – how much money are you prepared to receive as it comes suddenly into your life? Be honest with how much money you can imagine coming your way – and then see if you can stretch that amount out a bit, little by little, keeping it still within range of something that feels comfortable to you, using your stomach and body sensations as a guide. A simple rule of thumb for comfort levels is that if you're getting butterflies in your stomach, cold feet, or any other noticeable physiological effects, you've left your comfort zone. You can increase what you are comfortable with, but for best most immediate results, start with something small that feels most comfortable to you, and give yourself a chance to experience success with small windfalls first.

Answering these questions is an excellent energetic exercise for preparing yourself to experience these kinds of reality shifts involving money, while at the same time energizing money to become High Energy Money.

Fun with Money: Doubling Meditation

How do you feel when you check your bank balance and discover you have twice as much money as you thought?

Fun with Money: Windfall Meditation

What ways are you open to receiving unexpected windfalls in which money comes to you unexpectedly?

Energizing Money

Indigenous peoples the world over have long understood that *everything is energy*, and *everything has consciousness*. Starting with this worldview, we have an advantage when dealing with everything in the world, including money. Knowing that we are capable of carrying on a conversation with money... both in terms of listening to it, and talking to it, is a powerful way to open a new connection with money that can otherwise become closed off or blocked.

A large part of the reason you are currently reading this book is likely related to your having a desire for a better cash flow situation and/or a better overall financial situation. One of the very best ways to attain such a position is to first ensure your own energy patterns are supportive of experiencing such a reality, by:

(1) Hold a **VISION** of what it might be like to be prosperous,
(2) Feel genuine **EXCITEMENT** about living your financial dreams come true, and
(3) Take active physical **ACTION** to help make your dream a reality.

Involving your head, heart and guts as equal participants in this way makes a huge difference. It is easy to see someone who is misaligned chasing after something his or her heart is obviously not fully in, yet sometimes we fool ourselves. The key to success in energizing money starts therefore with more fully knowing ourselves.

Having good alignment between what we think we want, what we emotionally feel involved with, and what we are willing to do gives us a clear sense of what we can believe will be possible. When we know in our heads, hearts, and guts that we are 100% fully intellectually focused, emotionally dedicated, and physically committed to our dreams, we will achieve them. This is a step some people skip through rather quickly, not realizing how essential it is to have a dream we believe is possible for us to achieve – neglecting to notice warning signs and uneasy gut feelings. Rather than foist something on ourselves we find distasteful, it is our responsibility to discover what we feel good doing and being involved with, and what leaves us feeling completely disinterested and uninvolved.

When you think of a vision of something you'd love to experience, you can find out whether you've got internal resistance to this vision by closing your eyes, relaxing all the muscles in your body (you can start by feeling your feet growing relaxed and heavy… then your legs… and moving onward up your body to your head), noticing what kind of physical sensations you are feeling. Any tension or tightness you observe in your body is a sure-fire indicator that you are experiencing inner energetic conflict. When you learn to sense this kind of conflict inside yourself, you are gaining new information so you can revise your vision of your prosperity dreams, and check again to see how your body responds this time. Eventually, you will find a dream that excites you without causing inner tension… and that is a vision you can hold for yourself that you will not be unconsciously sabotaging.

Once you are feeling good about a vision with respect to your finances, you are ready to take the first step in energizing your money. This first step involves opening up lines of communication with it… in whatever way feels most fun and enjoyable to you.

What was your very first experience with money? Do you remember the first time you held or saw money when you were a child? What was your most memorable childhood experience with money? Chances are, your first experience with shiny coins and crisp bills felt fun and magical in some way – possibly with a sense of tremendous excitement related to what these coins and dollar bills could buy for you.

Getting back an innocent, pure sense of the potential value and intrinsic capability of money is helpful for clearing the energetic connection between you and money, so rather than projecting something onto money that it is not, you are able to see it, feel it, and smell it just exactly like it is. There is great wisdom available to you when you take the opportunity to feel a sense of trust and oneness with money, in order for you to experience one another exactly as you are.

One of my earliest childhood experiences with money occurred when I was a little girl playing with my sister and other neighborhood children out in our front yard. We had fun making crafts and sharing snacks, and some of us began bartering and trading these small items of goods and food. Some of the children wanted more crafts and snacks than they had the means to trade for, which gave me an idea. I noticed that play money would help make our game much more satisfying and enjoyable, so everyone would be able to get exactly what he or she wanted. I began printing up my own play money for distribution to all the children, and created bank accounts for them to keep their money safe in my small blue locking suitcase when they weren't actively engaged in trades.

As children played and traded and used the play money, I noticed that by providing this business service, I was making money, and of course by printing money I was also making money (by definition). *Aha!* In this amazing epiphany, I understood a great deal more about money than I ever had before, on a very deep level. I was amazed that the other children took our new play money for granted, accepting it as something solid they could rely upon, and only expecting as much money as they felt they could earn based on the goods and services they were able to provide. Some children were tremendously resourceful and brought out all kinds of good foods from their houses, while others were content to mostly be consumers of all the bounty. I was further amazed at how willing the children were to give me so much food and so many toys essentially for free – for the play paper money bills I created.

Games like this one provide us with marvelous learning tools that can help us simultaneously open our minds to new ways of envisioning our relationship to money and overcome habitual ways of thinking about money. When I first heard about Robert Kiyosaki's board game, Cash Flow 101, I was excited to purchase a copy of it to play with my children, in order to share with them the ideas presented in Kiyosaki's book, *"Rich Dad, Poor Dad."* What I learned from playing this game was very much what my parents had taught me while I was growing up: we are limited as to how much we can earn if we remain in the "rat race" as employees, where the main money we earn is from income earned for the work we do, turning our own blood, sweat and tears into cash. The Cash Flow 101 game shows how the employee mindset is one strategy a person can follow in their life, but there are ways to generate passive income as well. Passive income is money coming in to us that we do not need to labor hard to earn. We can improve our financial position most quickly by paying attention to our cash flow, noting the balance of income and outgo.

In case you are feeling that your past experiences and associations with money and prosperity have been less than positive, and that this fact might have something to do with why you currently feel financially challenged, there is some very good news. Not only is it possible to improve your future, it is also possible to improve your past.

The concept of bicausality is one that our physical sciences intrinsically depend upon, yet something most people are neither fully aware of nor conversant in. A simple way of viewing this is realizing that we change the past when we look back fondly on memories... just as we change the future when we look forward optimistically. Discovering your own ability to change the past can make a world of difference in your financial situation, and is therefore well worth taking time to better understand.

*"The past is a gift,
the future is history, and
this moment is a mystery."*

I recently heard the saying, *"The past is history, the future is a mystery, and today is a gift, which is why it is called the present."* While this may seem true from a mainstream perspective of reality, those of us who experience reality shifts observe something rather different. We notice that there is a kind of handshake going on between the future and the past – one in which our thoughts and feelings are constantly influencing the reality we are experiencing in this present moment right here and now.

First, we notice how the past is a **GIFT**. No matter what may have transpired so far in our lives, we will feel most confident and enthusiastic by recognizing the many blessings we have received from the entirety of our past. When we find ways we have grown and benefited from all the challenges and difficulties in our lives as well as the happy-go-lucky experiences, we can see that all experiences offer unique benefits when viewed from a grateful point of view. The resulting improvement in our own personal energy, or Qi, is simply phenomenal as we contemplate our good fortune. Rather than blaming people, situations, or events for what has gone wrong, we can be grateful we have survived and learned something valuable along the way. Studies show that people who realize how much better off they are than they might have been tend to be much more successful than people who feel victimized rather than fortunate.

Secondly, we can see how today is a **MYSTERY**. This moment, right here, right now, is a moment of all-inclusive, infinite possibility. With so many options to choose from, we can more easily switch gears from old habitual ways of thinking and acting to something fresh and new. We can best effect change in the world with an attitude of beginner's mind, in which anything is possible. Many of the world's greatest inventions have benefited from their inventors being completely unaware that some people considered their creations to be impossible. A state of open-mindedness provides us with the ability to switch gears and realities to those which are much more congruous with our true interests and desires... as we develop entirely new mental models and ways of thinking. Viewing everything playfully, like a child, has also been shown to boost one's creativity.

Third, we can note that our future can be viewed as **HISTORY**, as we envision desired results. We often observe that we get the best manifestation results when we do what star athletes do time and time again, by holding a clear and consistent vision (memory) of success in our endeavors. It also helps to note that we can reverse negative self-talk wherever necessary, in order to ensure better visualization of what we truly desire. These visualization techniques are so very popular for the very simple reason that they work. We can think of this as making a solid intentional connection to a desired "future memory" outcome that is particularly robust and stable, precisely because our mind views this vision as something predestined... of something we are completely confident will happen next.

For those who find these concepts fairly easy to comprehend, there is something "extra for experts," and that is the matter of taking the above concepts and utilizing them for both forward and backward causation. Bi-causality works using the basic principle of this present moment always being the MYSTERY, and the past and future switching between being the GIFT and HISTORY. We can start by feeling gratitude and thankfulness for the GIFT, and whichever direction in time we are shifting, we remember the HISTORY we are targeting as clearly as a memory.

This kind of reality shifting requires a kind of emotional alchemy, in which we become increasingly more confident simultaneously envisioning more positive futures and pasts. The difference between the emotions of remembering the joyful HISTORY we are targeting (in the form of a past or future memory) and the GIFT of feeling supported by the universe creates an energetic emotional change, which can be directed into what we are envisioning. When we consider what we wish transformed as a memory (HISTORY) rather than a wish that may or may not come true, we are confidently welcoming a future-remembered outcome envisioned as already complete, a fait accompli. This kind of confident envisioning tends to be much more effective than fixating on want, longing, desire and lack.

In the case of forward causation, we hold an imagined / remembered future in our mind's eye in the form of a memory. This works best by thinking of what is desired as being very much a "done deal," such as a parking spot we "remember" getting in advance of actually finding it. This historical future memory is powered by our feeling at joyful, grateful peace with gifts from all of the past.

In the case of reverse causation, the past we are shifting is what we remember as we recreate history with the energetic support of a grateful future. In this fashion, it is possible for us to have "always had" an extra $1,000 in our bank account, for example, because we needed to have that money in our vacation fund in order to take a vacation later this year.

The key to success in all forms of bi-causal reality shifting is our ability to clear out doubts and fears, replacing those emotions with love, joy, purposefulness, enthusiasm and confidence. We can develop these kinds of skill with emotional alchemy as we practice regular meditation, and learn to clear our minds of distractions and extraneous energies.

Most any kind of meditation that we practice on a regular basis can help reduce stress and improve our ability to experience a sense of peaceful balance. We can try different types of meditation out by combining a favorite way to relax (take a bath, garden, listen to music, go on a walk) with a favorite way to focus attention (observing our thoughts, observing our breathing, feeling energy flow through our body). Practicing such mindfulness on a regular basis is a way of strengthening our ability to live lucidly… to be aware of ways that our consciousness is regularly influencing the physical world.

Any time we start to think of ourselves or talk about failing or having failed, we can remember to take a deep breath, relax, and embrace the idea that everything works out for the best, as we ask the universe the open-ended question,

"How good can things get?"

Fun with Money: Clearing the Connections

Find a place and time when you can concentrate undisturbed for several minutes.

Stretch and sit or lie down comfortably, imagining you are about to discover new ways to bring money into your life.

Take a deep breath, close your eyes, and imagine a conversation with your money. Exhale slowly, feeling your muscles relaxing.

Imagine what you most wish to say to your money, and what you'd like to hear in return.

Talk to your money about your plans to fully share and enjoy wonderful experiences with it and others, generously and joyfully.

Money Self-Assessment

While some people think that certain individuals are simply better able to obtain and keep money, the truth is that just like any other natural talent, gift or skill, almost anyone can improve their fiscal abilities. Even a person who starts out with very modest means can envision, embrace, and take action to build up from a humble beginning to establish sizable reserves of financial equity. This means just about anyone can become rich!

It helps to know that there are many more ways to make and keep money than you have likely seen demonstrated in your family when you were growing up. When I was a little girl, I got a sense that money was earned primarily by my parents, who went to work each weekday to earn a living. Occasionally, they discussed investments in the stock market, and I got a sense that these investments were not consistently positive cash flow experiences for them. My parents taught me by example to pay bills and credit card debt off regularly, and to be aware of tax laws, making sure to pay taxes responsibly when they are due. When I was growing up, my father would jokingly quote Bill Earle's famous saying:

"If your outgo exceeds your income,

your upkeep will be your downfall."

This is truly one of the most basic and fundamental principles in cash flow – we need to have enough money flowing in to provide for what is flowing out. Financially responsible people make sure they are not going deeper and deeper into debt than they can afford to repay, and know the importance of increasing income when expenses rise. As basic as this concept seems, we can boost our energy level to a higher level by revising it to something much more positive:

> *"When my income exceeds my outgo, my upkeep will be downright easy."*

We now have a positively worded affirmation mantra we can say aloud, write down and post in viewable locations, and utilize as the basis for feeling relaxed and enthusiastic about our financial future. These words look great posted on the refrigerator, written on a note in our wallet or purse, or stitched on a needlepoint framed in the hallway. While the underlying concept remains unchanged, the positive framing of our anticipated future helps us raise our sights from the depths of a cautionary tale to much loftier heights of anticipated financial success.

I noticed while growing up that some of my friends' families seemed less confident than others about whether they would have the money required to cover costs of essential items, such as food, clothing, and shelter. In the 1960s most parents did not talk openly about money matters with children around, but the presence or absence of emotional tension in different families was an ever-present backdrop in all my friends' homes. The basic truth was that some of these people were more relaxed and comfortable with money than others.

The primary difference between someone who is naturally at ease with finding and keeping money and someone who isn't has a lot to do with their inner thoughts and feelings about money, and what kind of financial habits they've developed over time. People who have various internal fears about money and experiences associated with money will encounter challenges in their external experiences that match their inner concerns. People who have few fears about money are better able to "go with the flow," and find that even when they encounter setbacks, these obstacles are more like speed bumps in the road than concrete and steel walls. No matter what your current monetary situation is, you can move onward and upward most productively when you renew a sense of hopefulness, clear out your fears, and set realistic goals.

Knowing how we feel right now about money and our relationship and attitudes toward money can help us improve our relationship with money, so let's check out our current emotional set points by honestly answering the questions in the following Money Self-Assessment Survey.

Money Self-Assessment Survey

This following series of statements are designed to help you better understand possible challenges you are facing in your current relationship with money. Each set of statements corresponds to ways you might be experiencing difficulty positively

(1) **Envisioning** financial prosperity,
(2) **Feeling good** about money, and
(3) **Working effectively** with money.

Notice which statements seem to match what you've heard people say about money... or what you've sometimes thought. Make a note of each statement you have agreed with at some point, to get a sense of internal challenges you are facing in your current relationship with money. For each of the following statements that you sometimes feel is true, make a check mark on this page or a piece of note paper:

DISCOVERING MONEY ISSUES:

Challenges in Envisioning Prosperity
( ) *Money creates problems*
(X) *Money doesn't buy happiness*
(X) *I can only make money by working really hard*
(X) *I will probably never make all that much money*
( ) *There are money winners and money losers*
( ) *I'm destined to always be flat broke*
(X) *I live from one paycheck to the next*
( ) *I procrastinate & put off financial decisions*
(X) *I have no idea what money choices to make*
(X) *I don't know how to manifest money*

(X) I don't get good financial information
( ) Money is the root of all evil

Challenges in Feeling Good About Money
(X) Money scares me
( ) Having money feels like a matter of life and death
( ) I feel terrified I might never have enough money
( ) Rich people are stingy and/or mean
( ) I have bad luck with money
(X) I lack fiscal self-confidence
(X) I doubt my ability to achieve financial goals
( ) I dwell on my financial past failures
( ) Remembering money blunders depresses me
( ) I worry I won't always have what I need
(X) Friends & family don't want me to succeed
( ) I feel isolated when it comes to money
( ) I get no help managing my money
( ) I feel just plain dumb when it comes to money
( ) I can't talk with anyone about my finances

Challenges in Working Effectively with Money
(X) I have a negative prosperity self-image
( ) I pick on myself & beat myself up about money
(X) I don't have many choices about money
(X) I don't have enough information to make choices
( ) I often feel overwhelmed with bills and expenses
( ) I feel blind-sided & surprised by monetary events
( ) I feel burdened with financial responsibilities
(X) I don't know what I can do to move forward
(X) I don't have what I need to make money

__14__
Total Score

Add together and calculate the total number of the above statements that resonate to some degree for you, and you will have an idea of the extent of internal challenge you're facing right from the start. Most everyone will have checked off some of the above statements, due to the simple fact that most of us have grown up in families and societies that propagate some rather negative beliefs about money.

Total Score: 0 – 4
If you honestly scored fewer than five money issues listed here, Congratulations! You are an extremely rare and fortunate individual who is apparently doing very well financially with meeting your financial needs. Pay particular attention to whatever areas you did check off, as clearing these up can dramatically improve your overall prosperity.

Total Score: 5 – 9
If your total score is somewhere between five and ten, you have room for improvement, along with a good sense of how it feels when you are in a state of graceful flow with regard to money. You are able to achieve great things financially, and thanks to your desire to turn your finances around, you are capable now of more honesty, commitment and resourcefulness than ever before. You're a winner!

Total Score: > 10
If you checked more than ten money issues, you likely have felt rather hopeless about your financial situation. All is not lost! The very fact that you are reading this book indicates you are ready and willing to learn what it takes to become financially prosperous. This is a great opportunity for you to set goals for yourself to

turn this situation around, and start focusing on where you'd like to start making positive changes in your relationship with money.

Do you see how negative energies in your relationship with money could be hurting you? It is possible that even some of your most long-held beliefs about yourself are not so much absolute unalterable truths as they are protective defense mechanisms that serve to keep you from making mistakes with money by not even trying in the first place.

What we can learn from this self-assessment is how we currently feel about money on several levels. Just as psychologist Abraham Maslow wrote about a hierarchy of needs, our own doubts and fears at many different vibrational levels can be viewed as relating directly to how comfortable and confident we feel about meeting our most primary, basic needs at the lower vibrational end of the scale, all the way up to the highest levels of social contribution we are capable of making.

Fortunately, once we have identified areas where we have rather negative or unhelpful beliefs about money, we are well on our way to turning our situation around in a much more positive direction. Just as we learned to believe and accept (often unquestioningly) all these rather negative beliefs, we can learn to accept and believe much more positive ideas.

Managing your money has everything to do with developing High Energy Money habits and beliefs. Those individuals who carefully tend their savings, growing their holdings larger and larger over time, often state something much like the famed Oracle of Omaha, Warren Buffet, did:

> *"I want to be in businesses so good even a dummy can make money."*

This kind of investment confidence does not come from panicky knee-jerk emotional reactions about how to invest and move financial holdings, but instead has everything to do with being calmly informed about the nature of your investment options, and making carefully considered, clear-minded decisions.

What is Your Money Personality?

A set of questions you can use to determine your own unique monetary mindset is:

> *Do you prefer to not invest at all?*
>
> *Do you invest to not lose?*
>
> *Do you invest to win?*

All of us are investors of our own time, efforts, energy, and resources. How we choose to allocate these precious commodities tells us quite a lot about our money mindset and emotional comfort zones.

There are no right or wrong answers here, and sometimes it may even move from one general category to another at different times in our lives. According to Donald Trump in his book, *Why We Want You to Be Rich*,

> *"All the investor types have the potential to become very rich, even those who expect someone to take care of them."*

I love to focus attention on this idea – that all of us have the potential to become very rich. We can stay true to our basic personalities, and still succeed. Co-author Robert Kiyosaki, in the same book describes four other basic financial personality types: Employees, Small Business People or Self-Employed, Big Business Owners, and Investors. According to Kiyosaki, emphasizing:

> *"The worst quadrant to be in for tax purposes is Employees, simply because there is very little you can do to protect yourself from taxes. The quadrants with the best tax breaks are the Big Business and Investors quadrants."*

The good news for those of us who love to work with our energy and consciousness to shift reality is that whatever type of money personality we may have, there are wonderful opportunities possible! The key to finding them lies in keeping an open mind to new ideas, while feeling excited and enthusiastic about doing what is required to find and explore those possibilities in ways that delight you.

Fun with Money: Remember How You Got Rich

Find a place and time to relax and concentrate for several minutes undisturbed.

Stretch out, lean back, or lie down and clear your mind of any thoughts of the day.

Imagine you are meeting your financially prosperous future self.

Ask your financially prosperous future self how riches came to you, and listen and observe carefully to get any glimpses, words, visions, or explanations of how your future prosperity comes to be.

Improving Your Relationship with Money

Do you remember feeling tremendously excited and enthusiastic about making a big change in your life in the past, and can you recall a time when your life took a huge turn for the better? Remembering and feeling this sense of exhilaration can help jump-start your new and improved relationship with money, as you remind yourself you're about to find out just how good your relationship with money can get.

Now that you've gotten a chance to see the results of your self-assessment, you have a great opportunity to create a positive healthy perspective for how you think and feel about money in relationship to yourself. The process of clearing out any fears, doubts, misgivings and concerns about money is vitally important to your financial health and wellbeing, and it's the beginning of what promises to be a beautiful relationship.

If you can remember the joy you first felt when experiencing money as a visceral, physical thing, take a moment to close your eyes and remember just how those coins and bills smelled, how heavy they were, how they looked and how they sounded. Recall joyful times you've had with money to help reestablish a fresh starting point from an innocent, beginner's mind perspective.

If you never enjoyed such a good introduction to money, it's not too late! Find some shiny new pennies or some other small denomination coins and notice how they look and sound and feel when you hold them and roll them around in your hand. You can even hold dollar bills and imagine that they are as fun as play money.

Imagine yourself feeling completely happy and at ease with your finances, with a secure sense of economic well-being and faith that all your needs will be provided for, and quite a few of your non-essential but highly desired yearnings, as well.

For this next exercise, notice which statements feel most different from what you've believed in the past. All of these affirmations are tremendously helpful, so feel free to adopt any new sentiments you feel especially attracted to. Simply making time on a regular basis to say these aloud, while feeling relaxed and optimistic about your future can make a world of difference in your financial picture. Even statements that seem different from your past or current beliefs can become gradually more familiar, and eventually your set of financial foundational beliefs. Pay particular attention to the intentions that give you a boost of energy and a sense of positive excitement, as these can become your own personal High Energy Money affirmation statements!

HEALTHY FINANCIAL INTENTIONS:

Envisioning Prosperity
( ) *I have exactly what I need*
( ) *People help me make money*
( ) *Money comes to me easily*
( ) *I attract situations that bring me more money*
( ) *I have faith all is right with my finances*
( ) *Every money experience is a learning opportunity*
( ) *I enjoy finding creative new financial solutions*
( ) *I see making money as a game I have fun playing*
( ) *I learn about money as I go*

Feeling Good About Money
( ) *I feel confident that what I need will be mine*
( ) *I enjoy winning at the money game*
( ) *I often find new ways to bring money to my life*
( ) *I love remembering past successes & achievements*
( ) *I feel a sense of excitement setting financial goals*
( ) *I feel supported by those who want me to succeed*
( ) *I feel grateful for what I have*
( ) *I am excited to discover how I'll make money next*
( ) *I am proud of my developing financial acumen*

Working Effectively with Money
( ) *I actively manage my finances*
( ) *I sense when I need to make monetary choices*
( ) *I get inspiration that ensures my financial success*
( ) *I ask questions so I know what next to do*
( ) *I build supportive relationships with my money*
( ) *I donate to causes that do good in the world*
( ) *My money helps make this world a better place*
( ) *I feel in harmonious balance with my finances*

Did you notice some exceptionally different ideas here? If so, be sure to make note of them, preferably where you can see them on a regular, daily basis. The very statements that seem the most foreign to you are the ones that can allow you to make the biggest changes internally, so you become much more open to taking advantage of financial opportunities when they come your way.

You can experience profound changes in your money self-identity by making positive changes in your monetary mental mindset, and taking inspiration from the above affirmations is a great way to start. Feel free to add whatever other affirmations come to mind that you feel will also be supportive to discovering just how good your relationship with money can get… and prepare to find out!

The key to getting the most out of improving your relationship with money is keeping yourself fully aligned with money, from your head down to your toes… from your ability to envision financial success and prosperity, to your emotional enjoyment and confidence in having and making money, to your desire to take financial action and do good things with money in the world. Successful alignment with High Energy Money can be physically sensed in your body – so that you can feel joy and delight and an absence of nervous muscle tightening or tension. By noting which area you can improve most for best results… whether it's having a clear sense of envisioning your own prosperity, or whether it's feeling enthusiastic about making money, or whether it's putting your money to the best possible use… you can now make note of which statements you feel most comfortable adopting as your personal affirmation statements.

When you feel physical tension in your body, your body is helping you recognize ideas that are not yet easy for you to assimilate into your prosperity belief system. With increased familiarity, you may find yourself gradually opening up to some new ideas, and feeling surprised and delighted with seeing yourself become increasingly more and more positive about money in general and your own personal finances in particular.

Now that you're feeling better about money from a theoretical perspective, you can take a look at the results from your self-assessment survey in the previous chapter with an eye to how you can bolster the areas that need a little help. The most effective way to do this is non-judgmentally, so you can simply see areas where in the past you have had some challenges with money. Just as you would be kind to someone you love who is first learning how to do something completely new, such as ice skate, ride a bicycle, or learn to type, remember to be compassionate toward yourself as you set out to transform your relationship with money.

Confucius once said there are three primary ways we learn something important:

"By three methods we may learn wisdom: First, by reflection, which is noblest; second, by imitation, which is easiest; and

> *third by experience, which is the bitterest."*

Imagine the best place for you to be financially... and how that will feel different than your current financial situation. Would you consider becoming a Business Owner or an Investor? If you are interested in venturing into completely new territory, make time to meditate and reflect on potential new directions, and find mentors you can learn from, to make your learning curve a whole lot easier.

A big part of your transformation into embracing High Energy Money is your willingness to surround yourself with people who support your vision, whether they are already financially successful, or positive-minded and prosperous in other ways.

Fun with Money: Profit Statements

Take a look at all the Healthy Financial Intentions affirmation statements, and choose ten that you most wish could be true for you. Write each one down in your own handwriting on a piece of paper several times, until you can start to feel a sense that the statement actually *is* true for you.

Finding Money

There are several ways for money to find its way to you, and you may notice you have more control of some of these ways than others. You can earn money through your own hard work or the work of others, you can receive it in the form of gifts, awards or inheritance, and you can find it through pure good luck. You can also find money in the form of personal or business loans, which you can then invest in a business or asset for future returns for yourself and those who provided you with the investment capital. All of these ways of finding money can be highly enjoyable.

The song "Pennies from Heaven" is not all that far off the mark, when it comes to popularizing the concept that money can sometimes appear as if out of nowhere. Reading and thinking about other peoples' experiences with money reality shifts is an excellent way to open your mind to the possibility that money can come to you as if completely out of the blue… because such things really do happen to people. As you read this book, you can ask yourself how ready you are to experience such High Energy Money shifts yourself.

To stretch your imagination a bit, consider some of the folks who've not only won a jackpot once, but they have won *twice*. James McAllister, a 62 year old hydraulic mechanic, won two Georgia lottery jackpots on Valentine's Day 2009. "It was because of Valentine's Day. If it hadn't been for my wife, I probably wouldn't have won either time." McAllister paid $40 for his winning tickets that day, worth $255,000 combined.

In early 2002, one of my best friends told me she'd flown on an airplane seated next to an ebullient woman named Ellen Lockwood, who'd just won a $945,531 jackpot playing the nickel Elvira Mistress of the Dark Spooky Slot MegaJackpots Instant Winners game at Harrah's Rincon Casino and Resort in San Diego. What impressed my friend was that Ellen was on the airplane with a noisy crowd of people. Half the people on the plane were her family, who she'd just taken on a celebratory cruise. Perhaps such generosity on Ellen's part set the stage for what happened next. Later that same year, Ellen won the $1 million jackpot playing the Pyramid slot machines after only four pulls! At the time, Lockwood was the first person ever to win a progressive jackpot on the nickel $1,000,000 Pyramid slot machine system, and her double win at slots in the same casino and the same year was quite remarkable.

Dozens of people have reported money manifestation stories at RealityShifters, with some noting they often get just enough money exactly when they need it. This is an important reminder to us to envision the answer to the question, "How good can it get?!" with a focus on what we are allowing ourselves to imagine as the best possible financial reality we can possible experience.

2009 and 2010 were economically challenging years for millions of people around the world. With so much fear and worry publicized in the media, I noticed I was becoming stressed about money, even as I craved a vacation getaway to reset myself back to a proper prosperity mindset. In a year that I felt I might not be able to afford a vacation that would cost me $1,000, I realized it ought to be possible to simply have that amount of money appear there. After all, money in the bank is simply energy, and can be influenced by positive intentions and a willingness to experience such a marvelous shift in reality. I was delighted one day that year to discover that I indeed did have an extra $1,000 in my bank account… just exactly the right amount to start making my travel plans! While it was easy for me to imagine I could have an extra $1,000 more than I thought I had in the bank, I see that it could be just as easy to have an extra $10,000 or more… it's all a matter of what I think is possible, and how much I feel I really need. And perhaps the best news of all is that these positive reality shifts can happen even when one's local or global economy is suffering.

Over the past decade, I've received many glowing accounts of wonderful reality shifts involving money, many of which are reported in the archived issues of the RealityShifters ezine, and in the "Your Stories" section of the realityshifters.com website.

One man wrote how he found extra money in his wallet after he was absolutely certain he had only four dollars left… yet when he needed to purchase something, exactly the right amount of money was there for him to spend.

A mother of three wrote in to report what she considered a miracle; she initially had only $100 to spend to outfit her children for their annual weeklong summer vacation at Bear Lake in Idaho, yet after having said a positive affirmation that they would have "more than enough money" for their wants and their needs, the amount of money in her wallet kept increasing by $50 every time she checked, until it increased to $450 and stayed there.

These wonderful examples remind us how it can sometimes be easier to obtain High Energy Money in amounts we are able to energize… exactly what we need, right when we need it most. These tend to be times when clear envisioning of financial prosperity combines with feeling good about what that money is needed for, and often we feel fully motivated at such times to work effectively with money in a way that is in full alignment with our head, heart, and gut feelings and intuition.

I especially feel inspired reading true stories by RealityShifters readers in extremely energized states of consciousness who have experienced money coming into being exactly when needed, as it materialized before their very eyes. One man who had spent a weekend at a spiritual retreat in Phoenix reported having attained such a "blissful, joy-filled state," that money was materializing in his hand so he could give it to the cashier; "I realized I was creating the money with which I was paying her!"

One of the **most** important points to remember and do something positive about is that it is only possible for us to receive as much money as we have the courage to imagine ourselves receiving. The better we can energize our money and ourselves, the more financially prosperous we can become.

Other ways that money can come to us rather unexpectedly is in the form of new business that arrives effortlessly, or through receiving things that we need that help us bring money into our lives.

Many people have experienced phenomenal success in finding money by practicing methods for staying positively focused and energized, such as by utilizing affirmations first upon waking each day and when going to bed at night. We can take advantage of the power of these special times for accessing the hypnagogic state between waking and sleeping. This is the very special state of mind where the conscious and subconscious minds come together in such a way that we are most likely to uncritically accept new ideas and ways of thinking.

Finding Money Exercise

1. Create a list of positive intentions regarding money that use words to describe the kinds of ways you'd most

like to find money in your life. Only include words that describe desired outcomes, and refrain from ever stating anything you do not wish to create.
2. Begin this meditation at a place and time where you are so relaxed that you can drift back and forth between wakefulness and dreaminess, such as first upon waking in the morning, or at bedtime.
3. Imagine you are face-to-face with the Source of All That Is… or with the greatest imaginable presence of Love, and that in this extraordinary energy field, everything you contemplate will come true.
4. Focusing on one intention for the day ahead, repeat it over and over and over again in your thoughts, as you remain completely relaxed.

Prosperity Meditations

Daily prosperity meditations are a powerful way to keep yourself in a High Energy Money state of mind, and making time to do one or more prosperity meditations regularly can work wonders in your life.

I do three prosperity meditations each day as a form of course correction that helps me live a vibrant life… this is akin to taking care to check the rigging and sails on a ship on a regular basis, rather than just assuming "the winds will take me where I want to go" and thinking it will operate just fine on cruise control. Your life feels best when you take care to respond to the changes in the winds and tides, and you can tend to those ebbs and flows in the energy currents of life by meditating every day.

Kundalini Prosperity Meditation

Start from a sitting position, with good posture so your spine is straight. If you wish, you can sit in lotus position and put your hands in mudras, special meditative hand positions. Breathe in through your root chakra at the base of your spine... squeezing your sphincter muscles (the same ones to control your bladder when you use the bathroom... and all the other sphincter muscles such as women learn with kegel exercises). When you release your sphincter muscles, hold your breath as you visualize the flow of energy rising up along your spine and flowing upward, and feel that energy rising up within you as you focus your awareness on the question, "How good can it get?" Put the tip of your tongue up to the roof of your mouth; this helps you recycle your energy around your entire being. Exhale, and imagine your energy is completing a circle around the top of your head, and then back down to where it began at your root chakra, completing a full circle... revitalizing your energy body, your chakras and entire auric field. You can feel your energy field getting stronger and stronger with every breath. You can feel a sense of radiance now, with greater joy and a sense of tremendous possibility.

Wake Up Prosperity Meditation

This meditation starts when you first wake up, in that place between waking and sleeping called the hypnagogic state, where you can access the ability to master lucid dreaming, where you can see yourself and others as you really are, where you can see around yourself as if you're outside your body, and where you can sense yourself through all time... including past and future. Lying down is helpful for this meditation. This meditation begins by asking yourself, "How do I feel right now?" Often, the answer to that question is something that is somewhere that is fairly good... but it might feel a bit tedious... a bit boring... not that vibrant. YES! It's OK to fall asleep and wake up while doing this meditation... the point is to really get that sense of how you really feel at the core of your being. Next, take careful note of comparing how you're feeling right now compared to how you'd feel on your best possible day... in terms of excitement, anticipation, joyfulness, playfulness, creativity, enthusiasm, exhilaration, accomplishment and every other feeling of maximum joy in your life on the best day of your life. Breathe these wonderful high-level energies and emotions in your belly... in your Dan Tien chakra (located just below your belly button, or navel). Feel this energy for several breaths, bringing that feeling of love and excitement inside you to the highest level you can currently tolerate. The third step is to feel the energies of possible realities for the next twenty four hours... this is kind of like flipping through the energies as pages of a book of the next day... feeling how the next 24 hours can play out for you... until you find the day that feels best to you from your heart's perspective... feeling it in terms of their subtle energies. You are making this choice based on intention... based on your sensitivity to discern what the choices are that are available to you... based on your ability to synthesize the emotional aspects you'd love more of... and this brings you to the best understanding of what you wish to choose. When you make a choice based on how the next 24 hours can feel best to you... raise the energies higher to the level you were feeling earlier in your Dan Tien chakra. Finally, bring additional dashes of whatever energies feel best to add (like seasoning for a favorite soup) to the mix. You can do this by asking your angels and the archangels and Spirit to help bring these qualities to you. Feel the way the next 24 hours can feel to you... and then pay attention as you live it to see just how it turns out.

Walking Prosperity Meditation

Listening to spiritually uplifting music that you find especially energizing and empowering and full of love and vitality and vibrancy for life -- the music of the soundtrack of your life in a state of success -- begin the walk by yourself, walking briskly... and allowing your mind to dance through all the thoughts and feelings of the day. At the middle of the walk, be aware of the presence of divine source with you right here, right now. Really feel this presence of Spirit... of God. Take a moment to reflect on what you are here to do, and your commitment to Spirit that you are here to provide service to others. On the last half of your walk, start bouncing more on your toes, raising your arms up high with ecstasy, joy and a feeling of connection to spirit and purposefulness on your path and renewed commitment to service as you return to where your walk began. Visualize that all your angels and all of the archangels are walking alongside you, supporting you and assisting you in being your full realization of divine being in human form... feel their energetic support and presence by your side, as they wish for only the very best for you in all that you do.

These three prosperity meditations are incredibly powerful in terms of promoting feelings of self love and confidence, with a boost in trusting your inner voice and picturing yourself as confident, capable, deserving and empowered and courageous and strong. Doing the meditations help you come face to face with how you are choosing how happy you can be each and every day.

Fun with Money: Finding Money

Next time you are walking around a city street or shopping mall, or are in a store or shop, tell yourself that it's really easy to find money everywhere you go.

Notice if you happen to find any coins or bills on the ground.

Keeping Money

Now that we're doing so many good things to help ensure money will start rolling in, it's time to get ourselves ready for how we can best manage it, so we can hang on to the money we need. The idea of keeping money is perhaps better stated as a principle of balanced flow. This is to say that just as you inhale and exhale the air that you breathe in order to stay healthy and alive, so too does money come in to you and go out from you on a regular basis.

The idea of keeping money is akin to finding a harmonious balance between money coming in and money going out, with a constant sense that in any given moment, we have a reliable, stable amount of money available for whatever we might need, with sufficient additional cash flow to accommodate expected and unexpected additional expenses.

In their book, *"Why We Want You to Be Rich,"* authors Donald Trump and Robert Kiyosaki bluntly state that there is a tremendous and oft-overlooked price of having a low financial IQ. As Kiyosaki states, *"The reason why we write, speak and create educational games and other products is because we want people to become rich and solve their own financial problems rather than expect others to solve their problems for them. We both agreed that by giving people money, we only make the problem bigger, harder to solve, and more dangerous."*

From a reality shifting perspective, of course, we focus on the question, *"How good can we get at managing our money?"* as we understand that getting money is just the first step in a money cycle in our lives. Acknowledging that we will not only excel at attracting money, but also at putting it to good use in the world, helps keep us aware of the importance of keeping a hands-on approach to our finances. We already know the importance of managing our friendships, the work we choose to do, and our physical health… and while we often seek outside assistance from experts in these areas, true and lasting success usually comes down to our adopting good habits and practices. Money management is one more thing we benefit from learning to do for ourselves, and overall success with money comes from developing a healthy relationship with our finances.

Once you've got enough cash flow to comfortably cover your expenses, you may or may not have emotional issues regarding hanging onto an amount of it that feels right to you. Whereas some people have an "easy come, easy go" relationship with money, others are much more tight-fisted, and this is a matter of personal preference. Knowing yourself and your own comfort levels regarding money and savings is your best guide to what amount of nest egg you prefer to keep in the form of liquid, easily manageable funds, and what amount you invest in other ways.

It's especially important for people who come into large amounts of money very suddenly to make well thought-out financial choices. CNN has reported that two out of every three lottery winners burn through their cash in a period of just five years, and some even go bankrupt. This pattern seems to suggest that many people have an emotional reaction to receiving large amounts of money, and have focused more on envisioning scenarios of spending rather than saving such sudden windfalls. We can learn from this, and take time to imagine how great we will feel when we have sizeable amounts of money in our savings accounts or other forms of assets. Clearly, it is every bit as important to retain money as obtain it in the first place.

The one thing everyone needs to keep in mind for High Energy Money, regardless how stingy or generous, is that there is more energy with the money you have when you keep it moving and flowing. Water has more power when flowing in a river, rather than when it's sitting stagnant in a puddle or pond, and our money will do best for us when it can be put to good use for others in the world.

So how can you ensure that you when money is flowing, it's going to provide you with a stable basis foundation of savings that remains steadily available to you? The answer here is a combination of practical, logical budgeting combined with freewheeling energetic intentionality.

Budgeting

Even if you don't feel inspired or inclined to keep a written record of your itemized expenditures, you can still keep track day by day of how much you are spending, while also keeping in mind how much you are bringing in as income every day. Keep track of your expenses and income for at least one month, so you can calculate and estimate how these patterns look when extended out over a full year. You can now look to see if there may be one or two areas where you can trim expenses back a bit, thereby increasing your savings. For example, instead of buying a cup of coffee on the way to work, if you have one ready to take with you as you leave home each morning, you can save hundreds of dollars a year. Checking out movies on DVD from the library instead of renting them can also save you hundreds of dollars a year. When you notice how much money is coming in and going out, you can set conscious goals for income and outgo, as well as goals for paying off your highest-interest debts and increasing your savings.

Plan for Future Expenses

Retirement and children's college funds can be started as early as possible, so you have time to contribute to them over a long enough period of time that they can build up to sufficient levels. If you are saving money for a particular purpose, you can set up automatic savings plans with names that remind you of the energetic essence of what you are saving for, that helps you reduce any temptation to spend that money on something else. Envisioning things you are saving for that you are really excited about and looking forward to experiencing is helpful, so that you will feel great enjoyment as your savings grow, working effectively toward your savings goals.

Intention to Keep Money

Simply having the intention that you will end each day with more money than you began has a powerful effect on your overall ability to keep money. You can also set the intention that you will end each week with more money than the week before; you will end each month with more money than the previous month; and you will end each year with a greater net worth than the year before. These intentions can be stated aloud, written down, or simply thought in order to be effective. If you are feel a desire for optimal effects, you can do all three. Developing a strong sense of yourself as being a person who has healthy savings is a very important requirement for successful saving, as your subconscious self-perceptions ultimately determine how well you stick with changes you make in spending and saving. You can maintain new, positive High Energy Money practices by envisioning how this is the kind of person you are, as you feel good about developing a new relationship with keeping money, and think about specific things you can do right now that will help you with your saving goals.

Supporting Good Causes

There are tremendous psychological benefits of gifting to those who offer their resources and services to others. Our emotional involvement with our money is at its best when we feel genuinely proud of and pleased with the value our money brings to the world. When we make a promise to ourselves that we will support good causes with our money, we feel truly pleased when we have more money to do good things. Money provides us with ways to help others, and making a commitment to ourselves to share money helpfully with those we wish to assist gives us a big boost emotionally that helps us find that money in the first place. Since you may need money to make money, the amount you give away needs to be budgeted just like any other expense… but the difference between the energetic boost of donating and most other expenses is that donations can greatly boost your overall prosperity. And some such donations are also tax-deductible!

Smart Shopping

Learn to strengthen your purchasing power! There are many ways you can stretch the dollars you do have by doing some very simple things that just take a little extra time. Looking online on the Internet for sales and coupon codes before making each online purchase can save you many hundreds of dollars over time. Smart shoppers plan their spending, so they are less likely to make impulse buys. A good rule of thumb is to make purchases when prices are <u>low</u> (not just "on sale" but actually real bargains compared with typical prices), and shop alone, rather than with others who might tend to add more to your shopping cart than you might have budgeted for.

Gambling

Generally speaking, gambling is not a net worth enhancing activity for most people who are intent on keeping their money, unless, of course, they are professional gamblers who earn their living gambling. There are some exceptions to this general rule however, as some people learn to master games that feature skill in addition to chance, such as blackjack. When playing blackjack, one successful player I know explained the importance of always playing *high energy tables*. "I go where people are in good, high spirits… and I wish everyone good luck. If people at my table are sullen or quiet, I switch tables to one that is more positive."

I had success gambling on slot machines on a cruise ship a few years ago, when I had a clear need for an exact amount of winnings in order to properly tip the service staff. I asked my traveling companion if she knew anyone who'd been very good at winning at slot machines, and she said her mother had been very good at winning with slots. My friend and I were able to clearly envision a plan for success, as we decided to work as a team, with my friend feeling her mother's helpful presence, and my noting which slot machine her mother indicated for us to play next. We moved from slot machine to slot machine, steadily winning as we played those slot machines that had a feeling of High Energy

Money, and moving to a new slot machine every time that feeling changed. We were feeling very heart-centered and good about our reason for gambling, feeling how much the service staff deserved good tips. We worked together effectively, pooling our intuitive gifts quite successfully. We kept our winnings in a separate cup that was not to be played, and in a few minutes won the exact amount of money we needed to pay for tips, at which point we stopped gambling, having achieved our High Energy Money goal.

Pay Off Debt Before Investing

The smartest way to handle your money is by reducing the amount of interest you pay on loans first, before putting your savings into investments that pay returns. This may seem hard to do, but your overall goal is to maximize return on your money. Loans with low interest are fine, as long as you are making very good use of the money you are borrowing. Thinking of your personal finances more as a business can help you recognize the value of decreasing interest payments and expenses, and help you increase interest income and returns on your investments.

All these tips are intended as guidelines to help you build up your financial capital and equity over time. There will be ups and downs, and you can keep yourself financially healthy through all of them by continuing your financial education and learning from each experience. Long-term discipline wins the day; look at your savings and asset allocation regularly, and rebalance it according to a strategy you have chosen that fits your financial personality and long-term investment plan.

And most of all… have fun! Encourage yourself to feel really good about having increasingly more savings, increasingly more prosperity and funds. Developing a sense of joy in keeping money improves your ability to develop and maintain new habits that can reward you with having more High Energy Money in your life.

Fun with Money: Prosperity Money Jar

Get a jar or cup to place in the prosperity corner of a room (the southeast corner of the room), and contribute extra pocket change to that container at the end of every day.

Strengthen the energy of this corner of the room with whatever art you have that inspires a feeling of excitement, joy and prosperity. The traditional Chinese good luck prosperity symbol is a dragon playing with a pearl, but anything that reminds you of abundance and financial success will work fine.

Keep adding to your money jar, and enjoy the feeling of abundance as it fills to the top!

Growing Money

There are two main ways we can think about growing our money: one is the highly intuitive, right-brain approach which has much to do with managing internal energies to continuously improve our ability to take advantage of financial opportunities as they come our way, and the second is the rational, left-brain approach of systematically assessing and improving our financial portfolio. Just as we all have two hemispheres of our brains, and are capable of thinking both intuitively and rationally, so too can we benefit from enhancing both ways of thinking in order that we ensure maximal financial health and well-being.

Rational approaches to money consist of the types of advice most commonly found in investment magazines such as *Fortune, Forbes,* and *Money.* Since investment advisors sometimes seem to have viewpoints that contradict one another, I suggest you find your own team of financial experts, based on your sense that they can be good mentors for you. Look for investors who are consistently successful at growing their portfolios to a level that you would love to see in your own life, and learn from what they are doing. Investor Warren Buffett is recognized as being one of the most successful investors in recorded history, so observing and learning from his approach to growing money is something you might wish to do, or you can read financial books and magazines and pay attention to experts who present useful information clearly in ways that make sense to you.

Knowledge Based Investing

Warren Buffett advocates that investors put their money into businesses they know about and understand, which are well managed and honestly run. While the resulting portfolio of investments might not be diversified in ways some financial gurus would advocate, this approach has clearly worked wonders for Buffett's financial net worth, and therefore warrants admiration, respect, and closer study.

You can educate yourself about businesses related to your own areas of expertise and interests, starting with companies in fields you've worked in the past, or are interested in learning more about. Following your own unique areas of interest, notice which companies have a solid history of high energy in terms of creative solutions to problems, good management practices, and good returns on investment.

Diversification

Another way to utilize analytical approaches to investment is to invest in a variety of different things rather than putting all investment eggs into one basket. There are some wonderful ways to do this in the stock market, such as through exchange-traded funds (EFTs). The concept with such funds is that they track an index (which tends to be diversified), yet they can be traded like stocks and are extremely liquid (so you can sell them quickly as need be). What this means for you as an investor is that you can invest a relatively small amount of money in something that would otherwise require a much larger investment, to get the full benefit of diversification of your investment funds, thereby minimizing risk. If you'd rather invest outside the stock market you can diversify your investments in art, precious metals, and real estate. There are investment opportunities for every level of investor, so keep an open mind for finding new ways and places to invest your assets so they can appreciate in value over time, and you're sure to find some good ones.

Intuitive methods for growing money appeal to a very different side of finances. They engage our emotions, in ways that harness the power of our subconscious, and the "below-the-belt" energy centers in our body that give us a sense of passion in life.

Affirmations

The use of affirmations is one tried-and-true method for growing money, and is a relatively simple yet highly effective way to help yourself overcome your own unique areas of fears and doubts by creating statements designed to positively override the nagging doubts that otherwise can run roughshod over your hopes and dreams for financial success. Knowing how some of our inner self talk can effectively flatten our hopes and dreams, canceling out the energy wave required to bring new creations to life, we can overcome that internal negativity by creating personalized affirmations that uniquely address our own particular weak areas. The statements of Healthy Financial Intentions mentioned earlier in this book make excellent affirmations, and you can select the affirmative statements that you benefit the most from based on areas you'd most like to improve your relationship with money.

Switchwords

The people who found effective switchwords recommend using words like FIND and COUNT to help align your subconscious mind with absolute certainty that you'll be getting money. You're going to have so much money, in fact, that your careful attention and care will be required to keep track of it all! You can either write down these words or put them some place you will see them everyday, such as in your car, on your desk, or on the refrigerator. You can also put these words in your journal, and in daydreaming posters of what you'd like your life to look like. You can include them in PowerPoint presentations on your computer along with your favorite, upbeat songs and images of all you'd love to do with the money that is coming your way.

Keeping your language focused away from words like "if" and on words like "when" as you maintain a feeling of excitement, wonder, and joy is tremendously helpful to continuing to build up momentum for money to be flowing your way. Maintain a present tense in your verbs, to allow your subconscious mind to consider the possibility that your desired outcome is already manifesting in your life right now.

Feng Shui

Another intuitive method for growing money works with Feng Shui, the ancient Chinese system of attending to energies in physical spaces. Start by selecting a representative symbol for your prosperity and financial success, and place this picture, statue, piece of artwork or other beautiful and personally meaningful symbol in the southeast (prosperity) corner of a room. Acknowledging that your future prosperity is assured in such visual fashion provides your subconscious mind with a powerful daily reminder that all is well with your finances. The energy of this intention can be honored by taking a few moments each time you see your prosperity corner to feel appreciative and positive for all the blessings of prosperity in your life.

Gratitude/Prosperity Journal

Keeping a journal of what you are grateful for each month, what you are dreaming and daydreaming about, including places you'd like to go, people you'd like to meet, and things you'd like to do is a wonderful way to establish a strong connection between what matters most to you and what is happening in your life. I've had fabulous success with such journals, finding that everything I write down comes true as I feel better and better about moving forward to help make my dreams come true. There is a feeling of effortless ease that develops, as this journal full of positive energy first documents what is coming, and then describes how happy I am when some things I've envisioned (like a free laptop computer, a dream vacation, and better relationships with my family and friends) come into my life. The important thing about keeping these journals is that only positive, uplifting, energizing statements are written in them, so reading and re-reading these journals feels inspiring, exciting and delightful. You can include positive affirmation statements in your journal, and use switchwords, if you like.

Prosperity PowerPoint

A fun way to grow High Energy Money is by creating your own energizing PowerPoint presentation on your computer. You can start by finding photographs or graphics that encourage and enthuse you, and combine these graphics with a favorite song and uplifting words to create a wonderful PowerPoint slide show / movie that you can play regularly to boost your spirits and raise the energetic vibration of everything in your PowerPoint show. For maximum positive impact of your written words, you can include switchwords and affirmations for increased prosperity in your PowerPoint.

The ideas for growing High Energy Money shared here can be tried one at a time, or in combination with one another. It is possible to use all these techniques together, as they are complementary with one another. A great way to utilize these practices is to start by trying the ones you feel most interested in, as you pay attention to your results. You may find it helpful to keep records of your finances over time, and which techniques are working best for you.

Fun with Money:

Money Tree

Get a little potted tree to put on your desk or in your prosperity corner (in the southeast corner of a room or space), and decorate it with slips of paper with financial blessings and affirmations.

Conclusion

At a time when some people are saying we've reached "the end of money," it's obvious by looking to the past that money isn't so much coming to an end as it is undergoing a process of evolution alongside humanity. A healthy relationship with High Energy Money is one which invites us to ask ourselves just how we envision an ideal world in terms of exchanges of goods and services, and how we see our own prosperous future in such a world.

This is an excellent time to take a checkpoint and reassess how you currently feel regarding the energy of money. Are you ready to experience money on a much freer, more playful, more joyful high energy level than ever before? Whatever fears and doubts about money you may once have had, you can now imagine and intend that you will get all the help you need to easily, effortlessly find, keep, and grow money that brings prosperity, balance, and well-being into your life and the world.

The ideas in this book are fundamental for developing a relationship with High Energy Money. While the basic techniques are simple, it is vitally important to work with them regularly in order to develop new habitual patterns of thoughts, feelings, and behavior. When you do the "Fun with Money" exercises at the end of each chapter, you develop new intentional and energetic habits regarding your relationship with money. Reading and re-reading this book, and talking about its core concepts with friends who genuinely wish the best for you can help you achieve positive results with financial prosperity. Ask yourself:

How good can my relationship with money get?

Hopefully, you are now feeling inspired and enthusiastic about experiencing the answer to that question. Think about some of the ideas in this book for finding, keeping, and growing High Energy Money that inspire you to envision something you can do right now that feels good and helps you work effectively toward your best possible financial future.

And most of all… have fun!

Fun with Money: Best Possible Future

Ask yourself and the universe to show you just how good your future can get.

Close your eyes, and imagine seeing yourself a few years from now, enjoying a prosperous, healthy, balanced life

Bibliography

Atwater, P.M.H., <u>Future Memory</u>, Hampton Roads Publishing Company, Charlottesville, Virginia, 1999.

Davies, Glyn, <u>A History of Money from Ancient Times to the Present Day</u>, Cardiff: University of Wales Press, 1996.

Fisher, Mark & Allen, Marc, <u>How to Think Like a Millionaire</u>, New World Library, Novato, California, 1997.

Furness, William Henry, <u>The Island of Stone Money: Uap of the Carolines</u>, J.B. Lippincott Company, Philadelphia, 1910. Pp 93, 96-100.

Haggin Geary, Leslie, "From Rags to Riches: Yes, It's Possible to Go From Flat-Broke to Super-Rich," CNN.com, May 21, 2003. /Users/cynthialarson/Desktop/RSGhem2010.2.pdf

Hagstrom, Robert G., <u>The Warren Buffett Way</u>, John Wiley & Sons, Hoboken, New Jersey, 2005.

Kiyosaki, Robert T with Lechter, Sharon L., <u>Rich Dad's Success Stories: Real Life Success Stories from Real Life People Who Followed the Rich Dad Lessons</u>, Warner Business Books, New York, NY, 2003.

Larson, Cynthia, Reality Shifts: When Consciousness Changes the Physical World, RealityShifters, 1999.

Mangan, James Thomas, The Secret of Perfect Living, Prentice-Hall, Englewood Cliffs, New Jersey, 1963.

Maslow, Abraham, Toward a Psychology of Being, J. Wiley & Sons, 1999.

Miles, Kent A. "Cobb Man Hits Lottery Twice on Valentine's Day," The Atlanta Journal-Constitution, Feb. 20, 2009.

Price, John Randolph, The Abundance Book, Hay House, 1996.

Trump, Donald, How to Get Rich, Random House, 2004.

Trump, Donald J. and Kiyosaki, Robert T. Why We Want You to Be Rich, Rich Press, Rich Publishing LLC, October 2006.

Wattles, Wallace D. The Science of Getting Rich, Tarcher, 2007.

"Money Buys Happiness When You Spend On Others, Study Shows," Science Daily, March 21, 2008.

About the Author

Cynthia Sue Larson has a bachelor's degree in Physics from UC Berkeley and an MBA degree, and gained additional financial services experience managing information technology projects at Citibank. Larson writes, teaches and coaches about how our thoughts and feelings change the physical world. You can read and subscribe to her free monthly ezine, RealityShifters, at her web site **www.realityshifters.com**

Books & CDs by Cynthia Sue Larson

Reality Shifts: When Consciousness Changes the Physical World

Aura Advantage: How the Colors in Your Aura Can Help You Attain Your Desires and Attract Success

Shine With the Aura of Success

Karen Kimball and the Dream Weaver's Web

Aura Healing Meditations

Made in the USA
Columbia, SC
01 February 2019